Holiday Le...
Cookbook

Creative ways to eat Christmas Classics

BY: Nancy Silverman

COPYRIGHT NOTICES

My Heartfelt Thanks and A Special Reward for Your Purchase!

https://nancy.gr8.com

My heartfelt thanks at purchasing my book and I hope you enjoy it! As a special bonus, you will now be eligible to receive books absolutely free on a weekly basis! Get started by entering your email address in the box above to subscribe. A notification will be emailed to you of my free promotions, no purchase necessary! With little effort, you will be eligible for free and discounted books daily. In addition to this amazing gift, a reminder will be sent 1-2 days before the offer expires to remind you not to miss out. Enter now to start enjoying this special offer!

Table of Contents

Chapter I - Turkey and Ham Recipes

||||||||||||||||||||||||||||||||||||||||||||||||||||||||||||||||||||||||||||||||||||

(1) Turkey Stroganoff Casserole

Cook up a creamy turkey stroganoff casserole using leftover turkey.

Serving Sizes: 8

Preparation Time: 20mins

Cooking Time: 30mins

Total Cook Time: 50mins

Ingredient List:

- 1 (12 ounce) bag egg noodles
- 2 tablespoons butter
- 8 ounces mushrooms (cleaned, sliced)
- 1 tablespoon fresh parsley (chopped)
- ¼ cup all-purpose flour
- 2 cup low-sodium chicken broth
- 2 cups cooked Turkey (diced)
- 1 cup sour cream
- ¼ cup Pecorino Romano cheese (grated)

||||||||||||||||||||||||||||||||||||||||||||||||||||||||||||||||||||||

Instructions:

1. Preheat the main oven to 350 degrees F.

2. Bring a large pan of water to a boil, and partially cook the noodles, until al dente (they need to be soft, but not cooked).

3. In the meantime, while the noodles are cooking, in a frying pan or skillet, melt the butter. Add the mushrooms along with the parsley and cook for between 2-3 minutes, or until the mushrooms begin to soften. Next, add the flour.

4. Pour in the chicken broth and add the diced turkey, along with the sour cream and grated cheese.

5. Add the mixture to the al dente noodles and stir to combine.

6. Transfer the mixture to a 9x13" ovenproof casserole dish, and bake in the oven for 25-30 minutes, or until the turkey casserole is hot and bubbling.

(2) Leftover Ham Bone Soup

Once the party is over, and you are left with a big ole ham bone, make a pan of veggie-packed hearty soup.

Serving Sizes: 6

Preparation Time: 15mins

Cooking Time: 1hour

Total Cook Time: 1hour 15mins

Ingredient List:

- 1 leftover ham bone
- 1 tablespoon virgin olive oil
- 1 yellow onion (finely chopped)
- 3 garlic cloves (minced)
- 2 medium carrots (peeled, diced)
- 1 russet potato (peeled, diced) 1 onion (peeled, diced)
- 1 cup canned white kidney beans (rinsed, drained)
- ¾ cup frozen corn kernels
- ¾ teaspoons fresh thyme leaves
- 2 bay leaves
- Kosher salt
- Black pepper
- 1½ cups leftover diced ham

||||||||||||||||||||||||||||||||||||||||||||||||||||||||||||||||||||||||

Instructions:

1. Put the hambone in a Dutch oven or large stockpot and add sufficient water to cover the bone to around halfway, around 6-8 cups.

2. Bring to boil before reducing the heat and simmer for between 30-60 minutes, or until fragrant. The time will depend on the size of the bone. Remove from the pot and discard the bone.

3. In a large pot, heat the olive oil, over moderate heat and add the onion and garlic, along with the carrots and potatoes.

4. Cook. while occasionally stirring until the onions are translucent, around 3 minutes.

5. Add the ham bone cooking liquid, together with the white kidney beans, corn kernels, thyme, and bay leaves and stir to combine. Season well with kosher salt and black pepper.

6. Bring to boil, and reduce the heat. Simmer for 10-12 minutes, or until the potatoes are just tender.

7. Add the ham, stir to combine, and cook for 1-2 minutes, or until the soup is heated right through.

(3) Ham and Pineapple Fried Rice

Enjoy this Hawaiian-Asian makeover for holiday ham leftovers.

Serving Sizes: 2-3

Preparation Time: 10mins

Cooking Time: 18mins

Total Cook Time: 28mins

Ingredient List:

- 3 tablespoons dark soy sauce
- 2 tablespoons toasted sesame oil
- 1 tablespoon sriracha sauce
- 1 tablespoon canola oil
- 1½ cups chopped ham (chopped)
- 1 large red bell pepper (stemmed, seeded, cut into ½ "pieces)
- 1 medium yellow onion (diced)
- 4 green onions, white parts minced (green parts cut into ½ "pieces)
- 3 large garlic cloves, minced
- 1 tablespoon fresh ginger (minced)
- 2 large eggs (lightly beaten)
- 4 cups cooked long-grain white rice, cooled to room temperature
- 1 cup fresh pineapple (cut into ½" cubes)

||||||||||||||||||||||||||||||||||||||||||||||||||||||||||||||||||||||||||||

Instructions:

1. In a mixing bowl, whisk together the dark soy sauce along with the sesame oil, and sriracha sauce and put to one side.

2. In a large frying pan or skillet, preferably no smaller than 12", heat one tablespoon of canola oil over moderate heat, until the oil begins to smoke.

3. Add the chopped ham, red bell pepper, yellow onion, green onion whites, and while constantly stirring, cook until browned, this will take around 8-10 minutes.

4. Add the garlic together with the ginger, and stir until combined, for approximately 30 seconds, or until the garlic emits its fragrance.

5. Add the lightly beaten eggs to the frying pan and stir combine with all of the other ingredients; constantly stirring until the lightly beaten eggs are cooked, for 2-3 minutes.

6. Add the white rice-soy sauce mixture to the frying pan, stirring until incorporated and heated through.

7. Turn the heat off and add the pineapple and the remaining green onions. Serve!

(4) Turkey and Apple Salad

In only five minutes you can prepare a quick and easy lunch or snack to use up the last of the holiday season's roast turkey and cranberries.

Serving Sizes: 2

Preparation Time: 5mins

Cooking Time: N/A

Total Cook Time: 5mins

Ingredient List:

- 1 cup leftover turkey (cubed)
- ½ cup apple (cored, diced)
- ¼ cup dried cranberries
- ⅓ cup plain low-fat yogurt
- ⅛ teaspoons dried thyme
- Sea salt
- Black pepper
- 2 pita pockets

||||||||||||||||||||||||||||||||||||||||||||||||||||||||||||||||||||||

Instructions:

1. In a mixing bowl, combine the turkey, apple, cranberries, yogurt, dried thyme, salt, and pepper. Mix well to combine.

2. Divide the mixture between the 2 pita pockets and enjoy.

(5) Ham and Potato Rosti

Simple ham gets a culinary makeover with delicious potato rosti.

Serving Sizes: 4

Preparation Time: 15mins

Cooking Time: 40mins

Total Cook Time: 55mins

Ingredient List:

- 2 large Desiree potatoes (peeled, grated)
- 1 yellow onion (peeled, thinly sliced)
- 2 cloves garlic (finely chopped)
- 10½ ounces sliced leg ham (torn)
- 1½ teaspoons cayenne pepper
- Bunch flat-leaf parsley (finely chopped)
- Salt and pepper
- 1 tablespoon olive oil
- 2½ tablespoons unsalted butter

|||||||||||||||||||||||||||||||||||||||||||||||||||||||||||||||||||||||

Instructions:

1. Preheat the main oven to 360 degrees F.

2. Place the grated potatoes in a strainer and gently squeeze to remove any excess liquid.

3. Transfer the potatoes to a mixing bowl and combine with the onion, garlic, torn ham, cayenne pepper and chopped parsley, and season well with salt and pepper.

4. In a frying pan on less than 8" diameter, over moderate heat, heat the oil along with the butter, swirling to make sure that the base of the pan is evenly coated.

5. Add the potato mixture to the frying pan and pressing down gently; make an even layer of the mixture.

6. Reduce the heat to moderate to low and cook for 17-19 minutes, until the underside of the potato mixture is golden and nearly cooked through.

7. Transfer the pan to the oven and bake for 12-15 minutes, until the potato is tender.

8. Scatter with chopped parsley and serve.

(6) Turkey Cacciatore

If you decide to go for a large turkey at Christmas or Thanksgiving make sure you have a really good recipe for the leftovers.

Serving Sizes: 4

Preparation Time: 10mins

Cooking Time: 50mins

Total Cook Time: 1hour

Ingredient List:

- 3 tablespoons virgin olive oil
- 2 small onions (chopped)
- 2 cloves garlic (crushed)
- 3 (14 ounce) cans chopped tomatoes
- Splash vinegar
- 1 tablespoon sugar
- 2 teaspoons dried oregano
- 1 pound leftover roast turkey (shredded)
- 1 (4½ ounce) Mozzarella balls
- 2 fresh breadcrumbs

||||||||||||||||||||||||||||||||||||||||||||||||||||||||||||||||||||||||||||||||

Instructions:

1. In a frying pan, sauté the onions in the olive oil, along with the garlic until just softened.

2. Add the chopped tomatoes together with the sugar, plus a splash of vinegar and a little oregano, and then simmer until the mixture thickens, for around 20 minutes.

3. Stir in the shredded turkey and then transfer the mixture to a casserole dish.

4. Heat the oven to 400 degrees F.

5. Rip the Mozzarella balls into bite-size chunks and then scatter them on the breadcrumbs with a dash more pepper.

6. Bake in the oven for 20 minutes, or until the turkey is heated through, and the top is bubbling and golden.

7. Enjoy.

(7) Ham and White Bean Soup

Come home to a creamy and comforting ham and white bean soup.

Serving Sizes: 6-8

Preparation Time: 20mins

Cooking Time: 1hour 20mins

Total Cook Time: 1hour 40mins

Ingredient List:

- ¼ cup good quality olive oil
- 3 cups cooked ham (diced)
- 1 cup white onion (diced)
- 1 cup celery (diced)
- 1 cup green pepper (diced)
- 4 garlic cloves (minced)
- 4 cups vegetable stock
- 2 teaspoons cumin
- ½ tablespoons adobo seasoning
- 1 teaspoon oregano
- 1 teaspoon black pepper
- 2 (15ounce) cans small white beans (drained, rinsed, 1 cup beans set aside)

||||||||||||||||||||||||||||||||||||||||||||||||||||||||||||||||||||||||||

Instructions:

1. In a large pan or pot over moderate heat, heat the olive oil.

2. Add the cooked ham along with the diced onion, celery, green pepper, and minced garlic.

3. Raise the heat to moderate to high, frequently stirring, and fry until the onions are translucent.

4. Pour in the vegetable stock and add the cumin, adobo seasoning, oregano, and pepper. Stir well to combine, and bring to boil. Reduce the heat to moderate to low.

5. Using a metal fork, mash the 1 cup of white beans.

6. Next, add all the beans, mashed and unmashed and simmer for 30 minutes.

7. Enjoy.

(8) Turkey and Potato Curry

An aromatic curry is a great way to make the most of leftover turkey and potatoes.

Serving Sizes: 4

Preparation Time: 5mins

Cooking Time: 15mins

Total Cook Time: 20mins

Ingredient List:

- 1 tablespoon sunflower oil
- 1 large onion (thickly sliced)
- 1 green pepper (seeded, chopped)
- 2 tablespoons curry paste
- 2 cloves garlic (crushed)
- 1 (14 ounce) can chopped tomatoes
- 5 ounces water
- 10½ ounces leftover turkey (diced)
- 10½ ounces leftover cooked potato (boiled or roasted, diced)
- 2 tablespoons mango chutney
- Small pack coriander (roughly chopped)
- Naan bread (to serve)

||||||||||||||||||||||||||||||||||||||||||||||||||||||||||||||||||||||||||||||||

Instructions:

1. In a large frying pan or skillet, heat the sunflower oil over high heat.

2. Cook the sliced onion along with the green pepper for a few minutes, until the veggies are beginning to brown and soften.

3. Add the curry paste, and garlic and cook, while stirring for 1-2 minutes.

4. Add the tomatoes and 5 ounces of water. Bring to boil and allow to bubble for 4-5 minutes.

5. Reduce the heat and stir in the diced turkey together with the diced potatoes, and cook for an additional 2-3 minutes, then season with salt and pepper and stir in the mango chutney.

6. Scatter chopped coriander over the top and serve with naan bread.

(9) Ham, Leek and Zucchini Frittata

A light frittata with feta and ham served with onion marmalade is a great meal to add to your New Year menu plan.

Serving Sizes: 4

Preparation Time: 15mins

Cooking Time: 20mins

Total Cook Time: 35mins

Ingredient List:

- 1 tablespoon olive oil
- 1 leek (pale part sliced thinly, dark part discarded)
- 1 zucchini (thinly sliced, then each sliced halved into half moons)
- Salt and black pepper
- 6 organic medium eggs (beaten)
- 2 ounces light milk
- 3½ ounces sliced ham (finely chopped)
- 1 cup rocket salad (roughly chopped)
- 1¾ ounces feta (cut into ½ "pieces)
- ½ cup onion marmalade (to serve)
- 2 cups mixed green salad leaves (to serve)

||||||||||||||||||||||||||||||||||||||||||||||||||||||||||||||||||||||||

Instructions:

1. In a 10" frying pan heat the olive oil over low heat.

2. Add the sliced leeks along with the zucchini and a dash of salt and black pepper. Cook, while stirring for between 3-4 minutes, or until just softened.

3. In a mixing bowl, lightly whisk the eggs along with the light milk and season.

4. Scatter the chopped ham together with the rocket leaves and feta cheese in the frying pan over the leek mixture, and pour it over the egg mixture.

5. Cook over moderate to low heat for 8-9 minutes, or until the egg is just set.

6. In the meantime, preheat the grill to high heat.

7. Transfer the pan to the grill and cook for 3-4 minutes, or until the frittata's top is set and golden brown.

8. Cut into quarters and serve with a dollop of onion marmalade and salad leaves.

(10) Turkey and Ham Salad with Greens

After all the excesses of the holiday season, a fresh green salad made with leftover turkey and ham is the best way to get back to healthy eating.

Serving Sizes: 4-6

Preparation Time: 15mins

Ingredient List:

- ¼ cup vegetable oil
- 2 tablespoons white wine vinegar (divided)
- ¼ teaspoons salt (divided)
- ¼ teaspoons pepper (divided)
- 4 cups salad greens (thinly sliced)
- ⅓ cup mayonnaise
- 4 teaspoons spicy brown mustard
- ¼ teaspoons dried thyme
- 2½ cups cooked turkey (cubed)
- 2 cups fully cooked ham (julienned)
- 1 cup seedless green grapes (halved)
- ¼ cup green onions (thinly sliced)
- ¼ cup slivered almonds (toasted)

IIIIIIIIIIIIIIIIIIIIIIIIIIIIIIIIIIIIIIIIIIIIIIIIIIIIIIIIIIIIIIIIIIIIIIIIII

Instructions:

1. In a mixing bowl, combine the oil along with one tablespoon of white wine vinegar, 1/8 teaspoon each of salt and pepper, and toss with the salad greens.

2. Arrange the salad greens on a large serving platter.

3. In a bowl, add the mayonnaise, mustard, thyme and remaining white wine vinegar, salt, and pepper.

4. Add the cooked turkey, ham, halved grapes and onions, tossing well to coat evenly.

5. Spoon over the greens and garnish with slivered almonds.

(11) Italian Seasoned Turkey Primavera

After a few weeks of roasted turkey and veggies, it's really great to enjoy home cooked Italian pasta.

Serving Sizes: 4

Preparation Time: 15mins

Cooking Time: 15mins

Total Cook Time: 30mins

Ingredient List:

- 1 cup uncooked penne pasta
- 3 tablespoons butter
- 8 fresh asparagus spears (trimmed and cut into 1" pieces)
- ⅔ cup julienned carrot
- 4 large fresh mushrooms (sliced)
- ½ cup yellow summer squash (chopped)
- ½ cup zucchini (chopped)
- 1½ cups cooked turkey (shredded)
- 1 medium tomato (chopped)
- 1 envelope Italian salad dressing mix
- 1 cup heavy whipping cream
- ¼ cup Parmesan cheese (grated)

||||||||||||||||||||||||||||||||||||||||||||||||||||||||||||||||||||||||

Instructions:

1. Cook the penne pasta according to the package instructions.

2. In the meantime, add the butter to a large frying pan, and sauté the asparagus and carrot for 2-3 minutes.

3. Add the sliced mushrooms, chopped summer squash, and zucchini and sauté until crisp but tender.

4. Add the shredded turkey, together with the chopped tomato, Italian dressing and whipping cream and stir well to combine.

5. Bring to boil, while stirring and cook for 2-3 minutes.

6. Drain the penne pasta and add to the veggie mixture, tossing well to combine.

7. Scatter Parmesan cheese over the top and toss.

(12) Turkey a la King with Rice

A welcome change from casseroles and stews this dish is simple to make, and delicious with rice.

Serving Sizes: 4

Preparation Time: 10mins

Cooking Time: 30mins

Total Cook Time: 40mins

Ingredient List:

- 2 tablespoons butter
- 1¾ cups fresh mushrooms (sliced)
- 1 celery rib (chopped)
- ¼ cup onion (chopped)
- ¼ cup green pepper (chopped)
- ¼ cup all-purpose flour
- 1 cup reduced-sodium chicken broth
- 1 cup fat-free milk
- 2 cups cooked turkey breast (cubed)
- 1 cup frozen peas (cooked, al dente)
- ½ teaspoons salt
- 2 cups cooked rice (hot, to serve)

||||||||||||||||||||||||||||||||||||||||||||||||||||||||||||||||||||||||

Instructions:

1. In a large frying pan, over moderate to high heat, melt the butter. Add the sliced mushrooms, along with the celery, onion and green pepper and stir until just tender.

2. In a mixing bowl, combine the flour along with the chicken broth until silky smooth, stir into the vegetable mixture.

3. Pour in the fat-free milk and bring to boil.

4. Continue cooking, while stirring for 2-3 minutes or until the mixture thickens.

5. Add the cubed turkey breast, frozen peas, and salt and cook until heated through.

6. Serve with hot white rice.

(13) Leftover Turkey Casserole

A one pot, turkey casserole recipe that uses up all your festive fare leftovers in one meal.

Serving Sizes: 4

Preparation Time: 15mins

Cooking Time: 25mins

Total Cook Time: 40mins

Ingredient List:

- 2 onions (peeled, finely chopped)
- 1 apple (cored, chopped)
- 2 tablespoons olive oil
- 1 teaspoon dried sage
- 2 tablespoons plain flour
- 1 ¼ cups chicken stock
- 2 tablespoons wholegrain mustard
- 2 tablespoons runny honey
- 14-16 ounces leftover cooked turkey (shredded)
- 12 ounces leftover roasted veggies (cut into chunky cubes)

IIIIIIIIIIIIIIIIIIIIIIIIIIIIIIIIIIIIIIIIIIIIIIIIIIIIIIIIIIIIIIIIIIIIIIIIIIIII

Instructions:

1. In a pan, fry the chopped onion along with the apple in the olive oil, until softened.

2. Add the sage and stir for 60 seconds, then add the flour, while stirring.

3. Add the stock, a little at a time, followed by the wholegrain mustard and the runny honey.

4. Bring the mixture to a simmer and add the shredded turkey together with the roasted veggies.

5. Cover and simmer gently for 12-15 minutes, or until the turkey is good and hot.

6. Season well and enjoy.

(14) Roasted Gorgonzola Pears with Farro Salad

Leftover turkey, leftover Gorgonzola – no problem!

Serving Sizes: 2

Preparation Time: 20mins

Cooking Time: 25mins

Total Cook Time: 45mins

Ingredients

Pears:

- 8 ounces pecans
- 2 tablespoons pure maple syrup
- 1 teaspoon brown sugar
- Pinch of sea salt
- 2 ripe pears (cored, halved)
- 2 ounces Gorgonzola

For the salad:

- ½ cup farro
- 4 cups spinach
- ½ Spanish red onion (thinly sliced)
- 2 cups leftover turkey breast

Dressing:

- 2 tablespoons olive oil
- 1 tablespoon red wine vinegar
- ½ tablespoons pure maple syrup
- 1 teaspoon Dijon mustard
- Pinch of salt
- Croutons (to garnish)

||||||||||||||||||||||||||||||||||||||||||||||||||||||||||||||||||||

Instructions:

1. Preheat the main oven to 350 degrees F.

2. Heat a frying pan over moderate heat and toast the pecans, tossing for a couple of minutes until they begin to brown.

3. Add the maple syrup, sugar and a pinch of salt, stirring until all of the pecans are evenly coated, and the sugar is beginning to melt.

4. Transfer the mixture to a baking tray or sheet to cool.

5. Place the slices of pears in a skillet and crumble the Gorgonzola into the wells.

6. Put the skillet in the oven and bake the pears until soft and just warm, for around 20-25 minutes.

7. Meanwhile, cook the faro, until tender, between 8-10 minutes.

8. Toss the farro along with the spinach, onion and leftover turkey.

9. Next, make the dressing: In a small bowl combine the olive oil with the vinegar, maple syrup, mustard, and salt, stir well to incorporate.

10. Season the farro salad with the maple mustard dressing and remove the pears from the oven.

11. Chop the pecans coarsely and scatter them over the cooked pears.

12. Serve the pears over the farro salad, and sprinkle with croutons.

(15) Mac and Cheese with Ham

Are you thinking about what to do with the leftovers? Then make this cheesy classic dish from scratch. You will never go back to store-bought again.

Serving Sizes: 6

Preparation Time: 15mins

Cooking Time: 30mins

Total Cook Time: 45mins

Ingredient List:

- 1-pound elbow pasta (cooked, drained)
- ¼ cup stick butter
- ¼ cup all-purpose flour
- 4 cups whole milk
- 1 teaspoon salt
- ¼ teaspoons black pepper
- ¼ teaspoons ground nutmeg
- 1½ cups white cheddar (shredded, divided)
- 1½ cups yellow sharp cheddar (shredded, divided)
- 8 ounces ham (diced)
- ⅓ cup panko crumbs
- 1 tablespoon butter (melted)

||||||||||||||||||||||||||||||||||||||||||||||||||||||||||||||||||||||||||||||

Instructions:

1. Preheat the main oven to 375 degrees F.

2. First, cook the pasta according to the manufacturer's instructions until al dente. Drain and set to one side.

3. In a large pot or pan, melt the butter over moderate heat.

4. Add the flour and whisk for 60 seconds.

5. In a slow, fine stream add the whole milk, whisking continually to avoid lumps.

6. Cook, while frequently whisking for 3-5 minutes or until the mixture begins to thicken and bubble and season with salt, black pepper, and nutmeg.

7. Set 1/3 cup of white cheddar along with a ⅓ cup of yellow cheddar to one side. Add the remaining cheeses to the pot and stir well until incorporated.

8. Remove the pot from the heat and add, while stirring, the pasta along with the diced ham.

9. Transfer the mixture to 9x13" baking dish, lightly greased with butter.

10. Scatter the ⅓ cup of white cheddar along with the ⅓ cup of yellow cheddar (set aside earlier) on top of the mixture.

11. In a small bowl, combine the panko crumbs along with 1 tablespoon melted butter and scatter on the top of the mac and cheese.

12. Bake in the preheated oven for 25-30 minutes, or until the cheese is bubbling and melted.

Chapter II - Veggies and Side Recipes

||||||||||||||||||||||||||||||||||||||||||||||||||||||||||||||||||||||||||||||||

(16) Fluffy Potato Rolls

Believe it or not, adding a scoop of leftover mashed potatoes to this bread roll dough makes for extra fluffy and golden rolls. Perfect for dunking in a bowl of hot, hearty soup.

Serving Sizes: 36

Preparation Time: 10mins

Cooking Time: 18mins

Total Cook Time: 3hours 30mins

Ingredient List:

- ½ cup shortening
- ½ cup granulated sugar
- 2 cups whole milk (warmed)
- ½ cup leftover mashed potatoes
- ¼ cup water (warm, 110 degrees F)
- 3 (¼ ounce) envelopes dry active yeast
- 6 cups all-purpose flour
- 2 teaspoons baking powder
- ½ teaspoons bicarb of soda
- 2 teaspoons sea salt
- 2 medium eggs (beaten)

Instructions:

1. In a bowl, combine the shortening, sugar, milk, and potatoes. Set aside for a moment.

2. In a separate bowl, stir together the warm water and yeast, until the yeast dissolves. Pour the yeast mixture into the potato mixture.

3. Sift together the flour, baking powder, bicarb of soda, and sea salt.

4. Beat the egg into the potato mixture, followed by the flour mixture.

5. Wrap the bowl with plastic kitchen wrap; set aside at room temperature for a couple of hours or until the dough has doubled in size.

6. Shape the dough into golf ball-sized balls and arrange in a lightly greased cake tin. Set aside to rise again, until doubled in volume (40-60 minutes).

7. Preheat the main oven to 375 degrees F.

8. Place the rolls in the oven and bake for just over 15 minutes.

(17) Sweet Potato Spoon Bread Pecan Salted Caramel Sauce

Spoon bread is an indulgent dessert that is made even better with a homemade pecan caramel sauce.

Serving Sizes: 6

Preparation Time: 1mins

Cooking Time: 45mins

Total Cook Time: 1hour 15mins

Ingredient List:

- 2 cups leftover roasted sweet potatoes
- 1¼ cups brown sugar
- 3 eggs
- ⅓ cup whole milk
- ⅓ cup freshly squeezed orange juice
- 2 tablespoons vanilla essence
- ½ teaspoons cinnamon
- ¼ teaspoons powdered ginger
- ¼ teaspoons kosher salt
- Butter (for greasing ramekins)
- ¼ cup water
- 1 cup white sugar
- ¾ cup heavy cream
- 1 teaspoon sea salt
- 4 tablespoons unsalted butter
- 1 cup toasted pecans (halved)

||||||||||||||||||||||||||||||||||||||||||||||||||||||||||||||||||||||||||||

Instructions:

1. Preheat the main oven to 350 degrees F.

2. Add the sweet potato, brown sugar, eggs, milk, orange juice, vanilla, cinnamon, ginger, and kosher salt in a food processor, pulse until silky smooth.

3. Use the butter to grease 6 ramekins (4 ounces each). Spoon the sweet potato mixture equally into the ramekins.

4. Set on a cookie sheet and place in the oven. Bake for half an hour then set aside to cool.

5. In the meantime, add the water and sugar into a medium-sized saucepan and cook over low-moderate heat. Cook for 5-6 minutes, without stirring until the sugar dissolves.

6. Turn the heat up a little higher and bring the mixture to a boil. Without stirring, heat the syrup for another 5-6 minutes until it becomes a dark amber color.

7. Take off the heat and pour in the cream, whisk until combined.

8. Stir in the sea salt and butter, then the pecans, stirring until the nuts are coated in the sauce. Set aside to cool a little.

9. When ready to serve, spoon the sauce equally on top of each 'bread' and enjoy.

(18) Cheesy Potato Muffins

These cheesy potato muffins are a great on-the-go snack, ideal for those busy days.

Serving Sizes: 12

Preparation Time: 10mins

Cooking Time: 35mins

Total Cook Time: 45mins

Ingredient List:

- Non-stick cooking spray
- 1 egg
- 3 cups leftover mashed potatoes
- 1 cup Cheddar cheese (shredded)
- 3 tablespoons fresh chives (chopped)
- Sea salt and black pepper

||||||||||||||||||||||||||||||||||||||||||||||||||||||||||||||||||||||||||||||

Instructions:

1. Preheat the main oven to 375 degrees F. Spritz a muffin pan with non-stick spray.

2. Mix together the egg, potato and ¾ cup of the Cheddar. Stir in two tablespoons of chives. Season to taste with sea salt and black pepper.

3. Use an ice cream/cupcake scoop to spoon the mixture into the muffin pan.

4. Place in the oven and bake for just over half an hour.

5. Take out of the oven, sprinkle over the remaining Cheddar, put back in the oven for a final 3-5 minutes.

6. Allow muffins to cool before turning out of the tins and sprinkling with remaining chives.

(19) Stuffing Waffles

Transform dry leftover stuffing into moreish crispy waffles that are perfect for topping with eggs and leftover gravy.

Serving Sizes: 4

Preparation Time: 10mins

Cooking Time: 30mins

Total Cook Time: 40mins

Ingredient List:

- Non-stick cooking spray
- 4 medium eggs
- 4 cups leftover stuffing
- Fried eggs and leftover gravy (for serving)

||||||||||||||||||||||||||||||||||||||||||||||||||||||||||||||||||||||||||

Instructions:

1. Preheat a waffle iron to moderate-high heat and spritz with non-stick cooking spray.

2. In a mixing bowl, combine the eggs and stuffing.

3. Scoop a cup of the mixture at a time into the waffle iron. Close and cook for approximately 8-10 minutes.

4. Take the cooked waffle out of the iron and set aside on a plate. Repeat with the remaining mixture.

5. Serve the cooked waffles with your toppings of choice, such as fried eggs and leftover gravy.

(20) Christmas Crumble

Bring new life to day-old nut roast, vegetables and cranberry sauce with this comforting Christmas crumble, packed with all things nice.

Serving Sizes: 4

Preparation Time: 10mins

Cooking Time: 30mins

Total Cook Time: 40mins

Ingredient List:

- 2-3 cups leftover roasted vegetables
- 2 cups leftover nut roast (crumbled)
- 1 tablespoon heavy cream
- 3 tablespoons gravy
- 1 tablespoon leftover cranberry sauce
- ¼ cup plain flour
- 2 tablespoons salted butter (room temperature)
- ¾ cup Cheddar cheese (grated)
- ¼ cup rolled oats
- Sea salt and black pepper

|||||||||||||||||||||||||||||||||||||||||||||||||||||||||||||||||||||||||||||||||

Instructions:

1. Preheat the main oven to 400 degrees F.

2. Add the leftover vegetables and nut roast to a glass baking dish.

3. In a small jug, whisk together the cream, gravy, and cranberry sauce. Pour the sauce over the mixture into the baking dish.

4. In a medium bowl, use fingertips to rub together the flour and butter until the texture resembles breadcrumbs. Sprinkle in the cheese and oats. Season to taste with sea salt and black pepper. Scatter the crumble over the vegetables in the dish.

5. Place in the oven and bake for approximately half an hour, until lightly browned and golden.

(21) Pineapple and Potato Creamy Curry

This indulgent creamy coconut curry with pineapple and potato is far better than anything you will order from your local takeout.

Serving Sizes: 4-6

Preparation Time: 5mins

Cooking Time: 25mins

Total Cook Time: 35mins

Ingredient List:

- ⅓ cup water
- 3 garlic cloves
- 1 teaspoon fresh ginger
- 2 tablespoons sesame oil
- 2 tablespoons soy sauce
- 2 tablespoons korma powder
- 2 tablespoons olive oil
- 1 yellow onion (diced)
- 7 ounces cooked potato (cubed)
- 1 cup canned coconut milk
- 1 cup canned pineapple chunks (without juice)

||||||||||||||||||||||||||||||||||||||||||||||||||||||||||||||||||||||||

Instructions:

1. In a food processor, add the water, garlic, ginger, sesame oil, soy sauce, and korma powder. Blitz until you have a smooth paste. Set aside.

2. Heat the oil in a skillet and add the onion. Sauté for 6-7 minutes, until fragrant and soft. Turn the heat down and spoon in the curry paste.

3. Add the potatoes to the skillet and simmer, covered, for 8-10 minutes, until they are hot through.

4. Stir in the coconut milk and pineapple chunks, simmer for a final 5-6 minutes, without a lid.

5. Serve the curry with your choice of side.

(22) Deep-Fried Stuffing Bites with Cranberry Pesto Dipping Sauce

Cheeky little deep-fried stuffing bites are just perfect for dunking in cranberry pesto dipping sauce.

Serving Sizes: 6

Preparation Time: 10mins

Cooking Time: 10mins

Total Cook Time: 20mins

Ingredient List:

- Canola oil (for frying)
- 2 teaspoons whole milk
- 2 medium eggs
- Leftover stuffing (chopped into bite-size pieces)
- 1 cup breadcrumbs (seasoned)
- ½ cup raw walnuts
- 1 cup leftover cranberry sauce
- ½ teaspoons black pepper

IIIIIIIIIIIIIIIIIIIIIIIIIIIIIIIIIIIIIIIIIIIIIIIIIIIIIIIIIIIIIIIIIIIIIIII

Instructions:

1. Preheat the oil in a deep fat fryer to 350 degrees F.

2. Whisk together the milk and eggs in a small bowl. Brush the mixture onto each of the pieces of stuffing and then dip in the breadcrumbs to coat. Set to one side.

3. Add the walnuts, cranberry sauce, and black pepper to a food processor. Blitz until smooth. Pour into a bowl ready for dipping.

4. When the oil has reached the desired temperature, deep fry the coated stuffing bites for 4-5 minutes.

5. Place on a kitchen paper-lined plate for a few moments and then serve with the dipping sauce.

(23) Leftover Veggie Frittata

Give boring leftover veggies a makeover with this tasty and healthy frittata.

Serving Sizes: 4

Preparation Time: 5mins

Cooking Time: 15mins

Total Cook Time: 20mins

Ingredient List:

- 8 medium eggs
- 1 cup whole milk
- Fresh parsley (chopped)
- Sea salt and black pepper
- ½ cup stuffing bread cubes
- 2 cups leftover roasted/cooked vegetables*
- 2 tablespoons olive oil
- Shredded Cheddar cheese (for topping)

|||||||||||||||||||||||||||||||||||||||||||||||||||||||||||||||||||||||||||||

Instructions:

1. Beat together the eggs, milk, parsley, sea salt, and black pepper.

2. Stir in the bread cubes and vegetables.

3. In a 10" skillet, heat the oil. Pour the egg mixture into the skillet and cook for 2-3 minutes. Turn the heat down low and sprinkle over enough cheese to cover. Cook for a final 8-10 minutes.

4. Place under the broiler for a final few minutes before slicing and serving.

*Broccoli and cauliflower work best.

(24) Double Stuffed Mushrooms

Stuffing stuffed mushrooms, yes, they really do taste as delicious as they sound!

Serving Sizes: 6*

Preparation Time: 5mins

Cooking Time: 25mins

Total Cook Time: 35mins

Ingredient List:

- 1 cup leftover stuffing
- ¼ cup Parmesan cheese (grated)
- 2 tablespoons olive oil
- 2 tablespoons fresh parsley (chopped)
- 1 clove garlic (minced)
- 24 button mushrooms (stems removed)
- Parmesan cheese and oil (for topping)

‖‖‖

Instructions:

1. Preheat the main oven to 375 degrees F.

2. In a large bowl, combine the stuffing, Parmesan, oil, parsley, and garlic.

3. Stuff the mixture equally into the mushroom caps.

4. Sprinkle with a little extra cheese and olive oil.

5. Place in the oven and bake for just over 20 minutes.

Four stuffed button mushrooms per person.

(25) Mashed Potato Puffs

Your little ones will definitely ask for seconds of these tasty little puffs.

Serving Sizes: 8

Preparation Time: 10mins

Cooking Time: 30mins

Total Cook Time: 40mins

Ingredient List:

- 2 medium eggs
- ⅓ cup sour cream
- 1 cup Cheddar cheese (shredded)
- 2 tablespoons Parmesan cheese (grated)
- 2 tablespoons fresh chives (chopped)
- Sea salt and black pepper
- 3 cups leftover mashed potatoes

‖‖

Instructions:

1. Preheat the main oven to 400 degrees F. Grease an 8-hole cupcake tin.

2. Beat together the eggs and sour cream, then stir in the Cheddar, Parmesan, and chives.

3. Season the mashed potatoes with a pinch of sea salt and black pepper. Add the potato to the cheese mixture, stirring until incorporated.

4. Spoon the mixture into the cupcake tin.

5. Place in the oven and bake for approximately half an hour. Allow to cool before turning the puffs out of the tin.

6. Serve hot!

Chapter III - Cheese and Nuts Recipes

(26) Honeyed Persimmon and Baked Brie

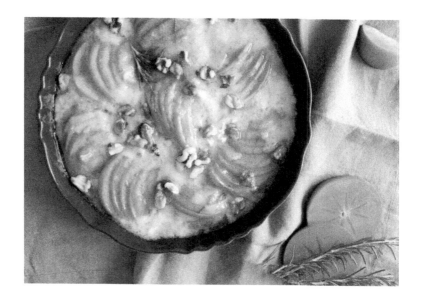

With poultry and meat taking center stage in the majority of festive meals, a lunch or snack that uses up all those leftover nuts and rich cheese is often a welcome change.

Serving Sizes: 10

Preparation Time: 10mins

Cooking Time: 32mins

Total Cook Time: 42mins

Ingredient List:

- 3-4 large ripe persimmons (peeled, chopped)
- 2 teaspoons rosemary (minced)
- 2 tablespoons walnuts (chopped)
- 4 tablespoons honey (divided)
- ½ pound triple cream brie (rind removed, cut into large chunks)
- French baguette (sliced, to serve)

||||||||||||||||||||||||||||||||||||||||||||||||||||||||||||||||||||||||

Instructions:

1. Preheat the main oven to 400 degrees F.

2. Arrange the chopped persimmon in a 9" baking pan. Scatter rosemary and chopped walnuts over the top and drizzle all over, with two tablespoons of honey.

3. Bake in the preheated oven for 15-20 minutes, or until the chopped persimmon is soft.

4. Take the pan out of the oven, reducing the heat to 350 degrees F.

5. Arrange the chunks of brie on top of the persimmon, nuts, and honey.

6. Return the pan to the oven and bake for a further 4-6 minutes, or until the brie begins to melt. Drizzle the remaining honey over the top of the cheese.

7. Allow to cool for 4-5 minutes, and serve with slices of French baguette.

(27) Parmesan Garlic Mashed Potato Patties

You will love these Parmesan potato patties. They are a great way to use up leftover cheese and potatoes.

Serving Sizes: 8

Preparation Time: 15mins

Cooking Time: 30mins

Total Cook Time: 45mins

Ingredient List:

- Nonstick spray
- 2 large egg whites
- ⅓ cup Italian seasoned breadcrumbs
- 1½ teaspoons garlic powder
- ⅓ cup leftover Parmesan cheese (grated)
- 2⅔ cups leftover mashed potatoes (cold)

||||||||||||||||||||||||||||||||||||||||||||||||||||||||||||||||||||||||||||||||

Instructions:

1. Preheat the main oven to 425 degrees F. Lightly mist a baking tray or sheet with nonstick cooking spray.

2. To a small mixing bowl, add the egg whites, whisking to combine.

3. In a second mixing bowl add the breadcrumbs along with the garlic powder, and leftover Parmesan cheese, mix well to incorporate.

4. Take a 1/3 cup measuring cup, and form the cold mashed potatoes into eight patty shapes.

5. Brush each of the eight patties with egg whites, and dip into the breadcrumb mixture.

6. Place the patties on the baking sheet and lightly spray the top of the patties with a little more nonstick cooking spray.

7. Bake in the oven for 15 minutes, or until the underside of the patties are golden brown; flip over and cook for an additional 10-12 minutes, or until golden brown on both sides.

(28) Cheddar and Walnut Soup

A couple of spoonfuls of chopped walnuts can turn a good cheese soup into a great one.

Serving Sizes: 6-8

Preparation Time: 8mins

Cooking Time: 10mins

Total Cook Time: 18mins

Ingredient List:

- 3 tablespoons butter
- 4 cups whipping cream (divided)
- 2 small cloves garlic (minced)
- 4 cups grated Cheddar cheese
- 4 medium egg yolks
- ¼ cup leftover cup walnuts (finely chopped)

‖‖‖

Instructions:

1. Add the butter to the top of a double boiler.

2. Pour in half of the cream along with the minced garlic and Cheddar cheese.

3. Cook over hot water until the Cheddar cheese is completely melted.

4. Combine the remaining whipping cream with the egg yolks, and add to the cheese mixture, while constantly stirring, until the soup is heated through. The soup must not be allowed to boil.

5. Ladle the soup into bowls and scatter with finely chopped walnuts.

(29) Mixed Nut Bars

Sweet and nutty bars are the just the thing to pop in your lunch box when the holidays come to an end.

Serving Sizes: 16-18

Preparation Time: 15mins

Cooking Time: 25mins

Total Cook Time: 40mins

Ingredient List:

- 1½ cups flour
- ¾ cups powdered sugar
- ½ cup butter
- 2 cups mixed nuts*
- 3 tablespoons butter
- 1 cup butterscotch chips
- ¾ cup corn syrup
- 2 cups semisweet chocolate chips
- 1/2 cup peanut butter

||||||||||||||||||||||||||||||||||||||||||||||||||||||||||||||||||||||||||||||

Instructions:

1. Using a pastry blender, cut the flour, powdered sugar, and half a cup of butter. Firmly press the mixture into an ungreased, unlined, 9x13" baking pan and bake in the oven at 350 degrees F for 12 minutes.

2. Sprinkle the mixed nuts over the crust.

3. In a saucepan, melt three tablespoons of butter, along with the butterscotch chips and corn syrup. Pour this mixture over the mixed nuts.

4. Return the pan to the oven and bake for an additional 5 minutes.

5. In a medium-sized saucepan, melt the semisweet chocolate chips along with the peanut butter.

6. Spread the mixture over the bars. Allow to completely cool and cut into slices.

*Measure the after you remove their shells

(30) Grilled Cauliflower with Winter Pesto

Use up those leftover nuts with a comforting and tasty family, veggie meal.

Serving Sizes: 4

Preparation Time: 20mins

Cooking Time: 45mins

Total Cook Time: 1hour 5mins

Ingredient List:

- Olive oil
- 1 onion (peeled, thinly sliced into rings)
- 1 cauliflower (stalks trimmed)
- 1 teaspoon ground dried chili
- Sea salt and black pepper
- Olive oil
- 2 (14 ounce) cans cannellini beans

Pesto:

- 1½ tablespoons unsalted leftover nuts
- 4 sprigs rosemary or thyme
- 1 medium lemon

|||||||||||||||||||||||||||||||||||||||||||||||||||||||||||||||||||||||

Instructions:

1. In a frying pan, heat a generous dash of oil and fry the onion rings for 12-15 minutes, or until crispy and golden. Using a slotted kitchen utensil, remove the onions from the pan, and transfer to a kitchen paper towel lined plates.

2. In a large pan filled with salted water over moderate heat, boil the whole cauliflower for 3-4 minutes, drain and set aside to cool.

3. Rub the cauliflower with chili, sea salt, and black pepper, drizzle with olive oil and set to one side.

4. To make the pesto: First, toasted the leftover nuts over low heat in a frying pan, until fragrant. Transfer them to a food blender or processor and process until combined.

5. Add the rosemary or thyme along with a dash of salt and once again, process until combined. Season with fresh lemon juice, olive oil, salt and pepper and set aside.

6. In a small pan and over low heat, heat the beans together with 2 tablespoons of bean juice, until hot, this will take around 8-10 minutes. Mash the beans and add two tablespoons of pesto, while stirring to combine.

7. Preheat a skillet over high heat.

8. Slice the cauliflower into quarters and char for between 8-10 minutes, or until charred and golden.

9. Equally divide the pesto mash between 4 dinner plates and top with a ¼ of the cauliflower, a splash of oil and crispy onions.

Chapter IV - Cranberry Sauce Recipes

||||||||||||||||||||||||||||||||||||||||||||||||||||||||||||||||||||||||||||||||

(31) Spicy Cranberry Salsa

If you like your food a little hotter, then you'll go crazy for this spicy cranberry salsa that pairs wonderfully with Mexican dishes.

Serving Sizes: 1¾ cups salsa

Preparation Time: 3mins

Cooking Time: 12mins

Total Cook Time: 15mins

Ingredient List:

- 1 teaspoon olive oil
- 4 garlic cloves (minced)
- 1 yellow onion (finely chopped)
- 3 serrano chilies (seeded, stemmed, chopped)
- ½ pound fresh tomatoes (seeded, cored, diced)
- 1 tablespoon leftover cranberry sauce
- 1 cup dried cranberries
- ½ cup apple cider
- 2 tablespoons fresh parsley (chopped)
- Sea salt and black pepper

IIIIIIIIIIIIIIIIIIIIIIIIIIIIIIIIIIIIIIIIIIIIIIIIIIIIIIIIIIIIIIIIIIIIIIIIIII

Instructions:

1. Heat the oil in a large frying pan over moderate heat.

2. Add the garlic, onion, and chillies. Sauté for 5-6 minutes.

3. Add the tomatoes, cranberry sauce, dried cranberries, and apple cider to the pan. Heat on a simmer for 5-6 minutes, while stirring, until the dried cranberries become soft.

4. Transfer the mixture to a blender and blitz until smooth.

5. Season with sea salt and black pepper and stir in the parsley.

6. Allow to cool before serving.

(32) Basil-Baked Brie with Lemon Cranberry Sauce

Gooey melted brie flavored with fresh basil makes a fabulous dinner party appetizer that guests can get really stuck in to.

Serving Sizes: 4

Preparation Time: 5mins

Cooking Time: 25mins

Total Cook Time: 30mins

Ingredient List:

- ¾ cup leftover cranberry sauce
- 1 teaspoon freshly squeezed lemon juice
- 1 tablespoon fresh basil (roughly chopped)
- 1 (7 ounce) brie wheel
- Fresh basil leaves (for garnish)

||||||||||||||||||||||||||||||||||||||||||||||||||||||||||||||||||

Instructions:

1. Preheat the main oven to 350 degrees F.

2. Mix together the cranberry sauce, lemon juice, and basil in a small bowl.

3. Set the brie wheel on a cookie sheet.

4. Spoon the sauce on top of the brie.

5. Place in the oven and bake for just over 20 minutes, until the sides of the wheel begin to bulge.

6. Scatter over a few leaves of basil before serving.

(33) Oatmeal and Cranberry Breakfast Bars

These scrumptious breakfast bars are packed full of oats, which will keep bursting with energy all morning.

Serving Sizes: 24

Preparation Time: 2mins

Cooking Time: N/A

Total Cook Time: 2mins

Ingredient List:

- 2 cups rolled oats (old-fashioned) variety
- 2 cups all-purpose flour
- 1 cup light brown sugar
- ½ teaspoons bicarb of soda
- 1 teaspoon baking powder
- ½ teaspoons sea salt
- 1 cup unsalted butter (chilled, chopped)
- 14 ounces leftover cranberry sauce

||||||||||||||||||||||||||||||||||||||||||||||||||||||||||||||||||||||||

Instructions:

1. Preheat the main oven to 350 degrees F.

2. Add the oats, all-purpose flour, sugar, bicarb of soda, baking powder, and sea salt.

3. Rub the butter into the dry ingredients using your fingertips. The mixture is ready when the biggest pieces of the mixture are the oats.

4. Press ¾ of the mixture firmly down into a rectangular cake tin. Dollop the cranberry sauce on top and then sprinkle over the remaining oats.

5. Place in the oven and bake for just over 25 minutes.

6. Allow to cool before slicing into 24 squares.

(34) Brie, Pear and Cranberry Pizza Bread

Cranberry, pear, and brie are a match made in heaven and are the perfect topping for a deep fluffy pizza dough base.

Serving Sizes: 8

Preparation Time: 5mins

Cooking Time: 40mins

Total Cook Time: 45mins

Ingredient List:

- 2 tablespoons virgin olive oil (divided)
- 1-pound readymade pizza dough
- ½ cup leftover cranberry sauce
- 1 ripe Bosc pear (sliced thinly)
- ¼ pound French brie (torn or sliced)
- Kosher salt

||||||||||||||||||||||||||||||||||||||||||||||||||||||||||||||||||||

Instructions:

1. Preheat the main oven to 400 degrees F. Use one tablespoons of olive oil to grease a rectangular cake pan.

2. Press the dough into the pan, making sure to reach into all of the corners.

3. Pour over the remaining oil.

4. Spread the cranberry sauce over the dough in an even thin layer.

5. Place the sliced pear on top, overlapping the slices in a single layer.

6. Evenly distribute the brie on top.

7. Place in the oven and bake for just over half an hour.

8. Take out of the oven and sprinkle over kosher salt before serving.

(35) Honey-Mustard Cranberry Sauce

This tangy sweet sauce goes great with everything; from BBQ chicken to hamburgers, it's our new go-to!

Serving Sizes: 2 cups sauce

Preparation Time: 2mins

Cooking Time: N/A

Total Cook Time: 2mins

Ingredient List:

- 1½ cups leftover cranberry sauce
- ½ cup American mustard
- ½ small yellow onion (diced)
- 2 tablespoons organic honey
- ½ teaspoons powdered garlic
- ½ teaspoons sea salt

||||||||||||||||||||||||||||||||||||||||||||||||||||||||||||||||||||||||

Instructions:

1. In a blender, add the cranberry sauce, mustard, onion, honey, garlic, and salt.

2. Blitz until totally smooth.

3. Serve with your favorite dishes!

(36) Cranberry Tea-Time Tartlets

Tiny little tartlets make use of both leftover pastry dough and cranberry sauce in a delicious way. Perfect served alongside a cup of afternoon tea.

Serving Sizes: 12

Preparation Time: 10mins

Cooking Time: 30mins

Total Cook Time: 1hour 15mins

Ingredient List:

- 14 ounces leftover pastry dough
- 6 tablespoons leftover cranberry sauce
- 1 tablespoon heavy cream
- Yolk from 1 medium egg
- Sanding sugar

IIIIIIIIIIIIIIIIIIIIIIIIIIIIIIIIIIIIIIIIIIIIIIIIIIIIIIIIIIIIIIIIIIIIIIIIIIIIIIIIII

Instructions:

1. Roll out the dough and cut into 12 (2¾" squares). Take a mini-muffin tin and press a dough square into each well.

2. Spoon 1½ teaspoons of cranberry sauce into each dough shell. Fold the edges over the filling and freeze for half an hour.

3. Preheat the main oven to 400 degrees F.

4. Whisk together the cream and egg yolk. Brush the mixture over the top of each tartlet and then sprinkle over the sugar.

5. Place in the oven and bake for just over half an hour.

(37) Honey Granola Parfait

Layers of creamy vanilla yogurt, crunchy honey granola, and fruity cranberry sauce, make a heavenly breakfast parfait or healthy dessert.

Serving Sizes: 1

Preparation Time: 5mins

Cooking Time: N/A

Total Cook Time: 5mins

Ingredient List:

- ⅔ cup vanilla flavor Greek yogurt (divided)
- 1½ tablespoons organic honey (divided)
- 1½ tablespoons leftover cranberry sauce (divided)
- Granola

||||||||||||||||||||||||||||||||||||||||||||||||||||||||||||||||||||||||||||||

Instructions:

1. In a large glass, or mason jar, layer ⅓ cup vanilla yogurt in the base. Drizzle over ¾ tablespoons honey. Spoon ¾ tablespoons of cranberry sauce on top and sprinkle over your desired amount of granola.

2. Repeat this process one more time, so you have six layers.

3. Enjoy!

(38) Cranberry Salad Vinaigrette

Put leftover cranberry sauce to good use in this fruity vinaigrette that will liven up any salad.

Serving Sizes: 1 cup dressing

Preparation Time: 2mins

Cooking Time: N/A

Total Cook Time: 32mins

Ingredient List:

- ½ cup leftover cranberry sauce
- 2 tablespoons good quality balsamic vinegar
- 2 tablespoons good quality olive oil
- ¼ cup water

||||||||||||||||||||||||||||||||||||||||||||||||||||||||||||||||||||||||||||||

Instructions:

1. In a blender, add the cranberry sauce, vinegar, oil, and water. Blitz until silky smooth.

2. Refrigerate for half an hour before drizzling over salad.

(39) Gingersnap Cranberry Pie

A vanilla cream cheese filling and cranberry sauce, sits in a festive gingersnap crust.

Serving Sizes: 8

Preparation Time: 10mins

Cooking Time: 10mins

Total Cook Time: 2hours 20mins

Ingredient List:

- 2 cups gingersnap biscuits (crushed)
- 5 tablespoons salted butter (melted)
- 2 tablespoons salted butter (room temperature)
- 8 ounces full-fat cream cheese (room temperature)
- 1 teaspoon vanilla essence
- Powdered sugar
- 2 cups leftover cranberry sauce

||||||||||||||||||||||||||||||||||||||||||||||||||||||||||||||||||||||||||

Instructions:

1. Preheat the main oven to 350 degrees F.

2. In a food processor, blitz the gingersnaps until they resemble sand.

3. Combine the gingersnaps and melted butter in a large bowl. Press the crust mixture into the base of a pie dish.

4. Place in the oven and bake for 8-10 minutes. Set aside to cool.

5. Beat together the 2 tablespoons butter, cream cheese, and vanilla until fluffy. Mix in just enough powdered sugar to thicken.

6. Spoon the mixture into the cooled crust.

7. Spread an even layer of cranberry sauce over the cream cheese layer.

8. Chill for 1-2 hours before serving.

(40) Creamy Cloud Pie

This adorable pink pie is creamy and fluffy; guaranteed to go down a treat with little ones.

Serving Sizes: 8

Preparation Time: 10mins

Cooking Time: N/A

Total Cook Time: 5hours 45mins

Ingredient List:

- ⅔ cup boiling hot water
- 1 sachet cranberry flavor jello powder*
- ½ cup chilled water
- Ice
- 1 teaspoon orange zest (grated)
- 8 ounces whipped topping
- 1 cup whole-berry leftover cranberry sauce
- 1 (6 ounce) graham cracker crust

||||||||||||||||||||||||||||||||||||||||||||||||||||||||||||||||||||||

Instructions:

1. In a large bowl, add the boiling hot water and jello powder, stir to combine. Set aside for 2-3 minutes, until the powder dissolves.

2. In the meantime, pour the chilled water into a measuring jug. Add enough ice to the chilled water to measure 1 cup in total. Pour into the jello mixture.

3. Stir the jello mixture until it thickens, scoop out any chunks of unmelted ice using a slotted spoon.

4. Use an electric whisk to beat in the orange zest and whipped topping.

5. Gently fold in the leftover cranberry sauce.

6. Chill for half an hour, until the mixture has become thick.

7. Spoon the chilled mixture into the graham cracker crust. Chill the pie for 4-5 hours before serving.

About the Author

Nancy Silverman is an accomplished chef from Essex, Vermont. Armed with her degree in Nutrition and Food Sciences from the University of Vermont, Nancy has excelled at creating e-books that contain healthy and delicious meals that anyone can make and everyone can enjoy. She improved her cooking skills at the New England Culinary Institute in Montpelier Vermont and she has been working at perfecting her culinary style since graduation. She claims that her life's work is always a work in progress and she only hopes to be an inspiration to aspiring chefs everywhere.

Her greatest joy is cooking in her modern kitchen with her family and creating inspiring and delicious meals. She often says that she has perfected her signature dishes based on her family's critique of each and every one.

Nancy has her own catering company and has also been fortunate enough to be head chef at some of Vermont's most exclusive restaurants. When a friend suggested she share some of her outstanding signature dishes, she decided to add cookbook author to her repertoire of personal achievements. Being a technological savvy woman, she felt the e-book realm would be a better fit and soon she had her first cookbook available online. As of today, Nancy has sold over 1,000 e-books and has shared her culinary experiences and brilliant recipes with people from all over the world! She plans on expanding into self-help books and dietary cookbooks, so stayed tuned!

Author's Afterthoughts

Thank you for making the decision to invest in one of my cookbooks! I cherish all my readers and hope you find joy in preparing these meals as I have.

There are so many books available and I am truly grateful that you decided to buy this one and follow it from beginning to end.

I love hearing from my readers on what they thought of this book and any value they received from reading it. As a personal favor, I would appreciate any feedback you can give in the form of a review on Amazon and please be honest! This kind of support will help others make an informed choice on and will help me tremendously in producing the best quality books possible.

My most heartfelt thanks,

Nancy Silverman

If you're interested in more of my books, be sure to follow my author page on Amazon (can be found on the link Bellow) or scan the QR-Code.

https://www.amazon.com/author/nancy-silverman

Printed in Great Britain
by Amazon

20187067R00079